MW00804814

FREEDOM AND THE ECONOMIC SYSTEM

FRIEDRICH A. VON HAYEK

Tooke Professor of Economic Science and Statistics
University of London

PUBLIC POLICY PAMPHLET No. 29

HARRY D. GIDEONSE, Editor

Martino Publishing
Mansfield Centre, CT
2012

Martino Publishing
P.O. Box 373,
Mansfield Centre, CT 06250 USA

www.martinopublishing.com

ISBN 978-1-61427-293-9

© *2012 Martino Publishing*

Cover design by T. Matarazzo

Printed in the United States of America On 100% Acid-Free Paper

FREEDOM AND THE ECONOMIC SYSTEM

FRIEDRICH A. VON HAYEK

Tooke Professor of Economic Science and Statistics
University of London

PUBLIC POLICY PAMPHLET No. 29

HARRY D. GIDEONSE, Editor

THE UNIVERSITY OF CHICAGO PRESS
CHICAGO · ILLINOIS

INTRODUCTION BY THE EDITOR

Could anything be more futile than the denunciation of dictators and the simultaneous support of the very policies that have made dictatorship inevitable elsewhere?

Is it mere accident that social-democratic Germany and Austria as well as communist Russia—which up to very recently were held up to us as examples of social advancement—have been the first to submit to totalitarian tyranny?

The air rings with eloquent defense of liberty. But—in Dr. Hayek's words—do we really know where the danger to liberty lies? What are the relations between the decline of the free market in economics and the growth of arbitrary power in politics?

This pamphlet is a distinguished contribution to our insight into this fascinating "no man's land" in academic specialization. It is an extension of a brief article in the *Contemporary Review* for April, 1938.

This is the twenty-ninth of a series of Public Policy Pamphlets which the University of Chicago Press is publishing. Frequently, the scholarly journals give no attention at all to problems that have an acute public interest, while the ordinary magazines can print little but superficial comment. The University might well perform a valuable service by making available to the public whatever special training and information it may have at its disposal. The continuation of such a series will, of course, depend upon its reception by the public.

Perhaps it goes without saying that the authors of these pamphlets are individually responsible for their views, and that they in no way involve the responsibility of the University of Chicago.

HARRY D. GIDEONSE

April 12, 1939

iv

FREEDOM AND THE ECONOMIC SYSTEM

I

Freedom and liberalism have become terms that are used to describe the exact opposite of their historic meaning. In a recent article in *Harper's Magazine* an author managed to speak quite innocently about "united action of all liberal groups under the leadership of the Communists." The editor of an American "liberal" weekly actually wrote in support of "taking communism away from the communists," but while these are striking examples, it is perhaps more characteristic of the collectivists of the left to camouflage under the time-honored liberal label.

The intellectual transition from nineteenth-century liberalism to present-day socialism, its extreme opposite, was made possible by one idea they had in common: the belief that the consummation of individual freedom can only be achieved if we break the "despotism of physical want."[1] If free competition from time to time inevitably endangers the livelihood of some, and if security to all could be attained only by restricting the freedom of economic activity, then that price did not appear too high. It would be unfair to deny that most of those who want to restrict private initiative in economic matters

[1] Cf. W. S. Jevons, *The State in Relation to Labour* (London, 1887), pp. 14–15.

[1]

do so in the hope of creating greater freedom in spheres which they value higher. So successfully has the world been taught to believe that "the socialist ideal of freedom, social, economic, and political"[2] can be realized simultaneously in all these respects, that the old cry of the opponents that socialism means slavery has been completely silenced. The great majority of the socialist intellectuals of our time sincerely believe that they are the true upholders of the great tradition of intellectual and cultural liberty against the threatening monster of the authoritarian Leviathan.

Yet here and there in the writings of some of the more independent minds of our time, men who have in general supported the universal trend toward collectivism, a note of disquiet can be discerned. The question has forced itself upon them whether some of the shocking developments of the past decades may not be the necessary outcome of the tendencies which they had themselves favored. Is it mere accident that the continuous expansion of the powers of the state, which they had welcomed as an instrument to bring about greater justice, has in so many countries brought the disappearance of all personal freedom and the end of all justice? Is it mere chance that the very countries which until comparatively recently were regarded as socially most advanced and as examples worthy of imitation were the first to succumb to real despotism? Or is this development not, perhaps, the unforeseen but inevitable outcome of those very efforts to make the fate of the indi-

[2] The *Times* (London) of July 16, 1936, in a review of J. Nehru, *India and the World*.

vidual less dependent on impersonal and perhaps accidental forces and more subject to conscious human control?

There are many features of our situation which strongly suggest that this may be so and that the attempt to realize some of the most cherished and widely held ambitions of our time has led us along a path which is fatal to the preservation of greater achievements of the past. The similarity of many of the most characteristic features of the "fascist" and "communist" regimes is becoming steadily more obvious. Not a few of the more advanced intellectual leaders of socialism have openly admitted that the attainment of their ends is not possible without a thorough curtailment of individual liberty. The intellectual past of the authoritarian leaders as well as the fact that in the fascist states a socialist is often regarded as a potential recruit, while the liberal of the old school is recognized as the arch-enemy, point to a filiation of ideas which is very different from that commonly assumed.

Above all, however, the effects of the gradual advance toward collectivism in the countries which still cherish the tradition of liberty in their social and political institutions, provide ample food for thought. The complaint about the "new despotism" of bureaucracy may have been exaggerated and premature. But anyone who has had an opportunity to watch at close range the intellectual evolution of the countries which eventually succumbed to authoritarianism cannot fail to observe a very similar development in a much less advanced stage in the countries which are yet free. And many changes, which in themselves look innocent enough, assume an entirely different aspect if seen in that setting.

There is much talk about the "dangers to liberty," and professed readiness to "defend" it against the wicked designs of sinister interests. But are we certain that we know exactly where the danger to liberty lies? Ought we not at least to pause and ask whether the menace may not have its roots in our own ambitions and endeavors? Is it as evident as many believe that the rise of the fascist regimes was simply an intellectual reaction fomented by those whose privileges were threatened by social progress? It is, of course, true that the direction of affairs in those countries has been taken out of the hands of the working classes and has been placed in those of a more efficient oligarchy. But have the new rulers not taken over the fundamental ideas and methods of their socialist and communist opponents, and simply turned them to their own ends?[3]

The fateful possibilities which such analysis suggests deserve further attention. If the suspicion should prove right that the expansion of state control over economic life, which is so generally wanted, should necessarily

[3] Long before the rise of fascism Marxist socialism made politics a question of Weltanschauung. Long before they were imitated by their opponents, socialists attempted to penetrate every department of life with their political organizations and to make arts and sports, no less than the forms of personal intercourse, a question of political doctrine. It was they who began to organize children of the tenderest age in political clubs, and who made sure that the people enjoyed their football and hiking no less than their theater and music only in socialist organizations. The armed political troops for the "protection of their meetings" no less than the specific methods of greeting among the comrades were first developed by them. *Ballilla* and *Hitler jugend*, *Dopolavoro* and *Kraft durch Freude*, and even the fascist militia and the S.A., are direct descendants of their socialist prototypes.

[4]

lead to the suppression of intellectual and cultural freedom, it would mean that we are witnessing one of the greatest tragedies in the history of the human race: more and more people are being driven by their indignation about the suppression of political and intellectual freedom in some countries to join the very forces which make the ultimate suppression of their own freedom inevitable. It would mean that many of the most active and sincere advocates of intellectual freedom are in effect its worst enemies, much more dangerous than its avowed opponents, because they bring to the collectivist movement which will ultimately destroy intellectual as well as economic freedom the support of those who would recoil in horror if they understood these consequences.

It is, of course, not a new idea that the central direction of economic activity might involve the destruction of freedom and of democratic institutions. This has often been dogmatically asserted and even more often been vehemently denied. In a recent symposium on "planned society" we find author after author concerned about this problem, either repeating the charge or attempting to refute it.[4] Indeed, Professor Gustav Cassel states his apprehension there with a clarity which leaves nothing to be desired. He writes:

Planned Economy will always tend to develop into Dictatorship . . . . [because] experience has shown that representative

[4] Findlay Mackenzie (editor), *Planned Society, Yesterday, Today, Tomorrow* (New York, 1937). A symposium by thirty-five economists, sociologists, and statesmen. See particularly the articles by H. D. Lasswell, D. Mitrany, and Sidney Hook in Part IV and the editor's prefatory note to Professor Lasswell's article which concludes that "freedom can never have the same meaning in a planned society that it once had or pretended to have in an automatic economy."

[5]

bodies are unable to fulfil all the multitudinous functions connected with economic leadership without becoming more and more involved in the struggle between competing interests with the consequence of a moral decay ending in party—if not individual—corruption. The parliamentary system can be saved only by wise and deliberate restrictions of the functions of parliament. Economic dictatorship is much more dangerous than people believe. Once authoritative control has been established, it will not always be possible to limit it to the economic domain.[5]

It will be useful to inquire whether this must necessarily be so or whether, as even Professor Cassel half suggests, the coincidence is accidental.

A careful examination of the transition undergone by countries which only recently seemed the most "advanced" in the social and political sphere and which have now passed into a stage which we are inclined to associate with the distant past, actually reveals a pattern of development which suggests that these were not unfortunate historical accidents but that a similarity of methods applied to achieve ideal ends, which were approved by almost all men of good will, was bound to produce entirely unanticipated consequences. An attempt will be made here to bring out these connections which can be traced between economic planning and dictatorship and to show why they must be regarded as a more or less inevitable pattern, dictated by characteristics that are interwoven with the very idea of a planned society.

The main point is very simple. It is that comprehen-

[5] *From Protectionism through Planned Economy to Dictatorship.* Cobden Memorial Lecture delivered in London, May 10, 1934, and reprinted in *Planned Society*, pp. 775–98, particularly pp. 797–98.

sive economic planning, which is regarded as necessary to organize economic activity on more rational and efficient lines, presupposes a much more complete agreement on the relative importance of the different social ends than actually exists, and that in consequence, in order to be able to plan, the planning authority must impose upon the people the detailed code of values that is lacking. To impose such detail means more than merely reading such a detailed code into the vague general formulas which people are sometimes willing to accept fairly easily. The people must be made to believe in the particularized code of values, because the success or failure of the planning authority will in two different ways depend on whether it succeeds in creating that belief. On the one hand, it will only secure the necessary enthusiastic support if the people believe in the ends which the plan serves; and, on the other hand, the outcome will only be regarded as successful if the ends achieved are generally regarded as the right ones.

II

A fuller exposition must begin with the problems which arise when a democracy embarks upon a course of economic planning. Although the full political consequences of planning will generally only reveal themselves after it has led to the destruction of democracy, it is during that process of transition that it can best be seen why personal freedom and central direction of economic affairs are irreconcilable and where the conflict arises.

Before we can turn to that task it is, however, necessary to clear away the mist of confusion and ambiguity which enshrouds the term "planning." Unless we are very careful in this respect there is great danger that the vagueness of the term will lead to argument at cross-purposes and that the real source of the danger we are facing will be misunderstood. Incidentally, these reflections will also enable us to draw a somewhat sharper distinction between the true liberalism which, it will be argued, is alone compatible with freedom, and socialism and collectivism in all their forms which—as the argument will show—cannot be reconciled with free and democratic institutions.

The confusion about which we speak is particularly dangerous because planning in the strict sense, about which the whole controversy turns, owes its wide appeal largely to the fact that the same word, "planning," is also applied to describe the application of reason to social problems in general—which is, of course, indispensable if we want to deal with these matters intelligently and to which it is impossible to object on rational grounds. The appeal to reason which the word "planning" carries with it because of this second connotation probably accounts for a good deal of its popularity when it is used loosely. Yet there is a world of difference between economic planning in the narrow sense of the term and the application of reason to social problems in general.

We can "plan" a system of general rules, equally applicable to all people and intended to be permanent (even if subject to revision with the growth of knowledge), which provides an institutional framework within which the decisions as to what to do and how to earn a

[8]

living are left to the individuals. In other words, we can plan a system in which individual initiative is given the widest possible scope and the best opportunity to bring about effective co-ordination of individual effort.[6] Or we can "plan" in the sense that the concrete action of the different individuals, the part each person is to play in the social process of production—what he is to do and how he is to do it—is decided by the planning agency. Planning in the first sense means that the direction of production is brought about by the free combination of the knowledge of all participants, with prices conveying to each the information which helps him to bring his actions in relation to those of others.[7] The planning of the planners of our time, however—the central direction according to some preconceived social blueprint—involves the idea that some body of people, in the last instance some individual mind, decides for the people what they have to do at each moment.

While this distinction between the construction of a rational system of law, under the rule of which people are free to follow their preferences, and a system of specific orders and prohibitions is clear enough as a general principle, it is not easy to define it exactly and sometimes even very difficult to apply it to a concrete case.[8] This difficulty has undoubtedly contributed further to

[6] On the liberal "plan," see in particular L. C. Robbins, *Economic Planning and International Order* (1937), *passim*.

[7] On the whole question of the "combination of knowledge" in a competitive system and the significance of competitive equilibrium I may, perhaps, be allowed to refer to my own article on "Economics and Knowledge," *Economica*, February, 1937.

[8] Cf. Walter Lippmann, *The Good Society* (1937), *passim*.

confuse the distinction between planning for freedom and planning for constant interference. And while an attempt to provide a satisfactory discussion of this question would clearly exceed the limits of the present sketch, it is essential to develop this crucial distinction somewhat farther.

By the construction of a rational framework of general and permanent rules, a mechanism is created through which production is to be directed, but no decision is consciously made about the ends to which it is directed. The rules aim mainly at the elimination of avoidable uncertainty[9] by establishing principles from which it can be ascertained who at any moment has the disposition over particular resources, and of unnecessary error by the prevention of deception and fraud. These rules are not made, however, in the expectation that A will be benefited and that B will be harmed by them. Both will be able to choose their position under the law and both will find themselves in a better position than would be the case if no law existed. These rules (of civil and criminal law) are general not only in the sense that they apply equally to all people, but also in the sense that they are instrumental in helping people to achieve their various individual ends, so that in the long run everybody has a chance to profit from their existence. The very fact that the incidence of their effects on dif-

[9] The stress is here on *avoidable uncertainty*, such as that by deliberate deception and wilful nonfulfilment of contracts. The elimination of such uncertainty must not be confused with the attempts to make changes like advances of knowledge, which have actually occurred and altered the existing opportunities, ineffective by preventing people from adjusting themselves to them. Although this is often regarded as a task of planning, it is certainly a bad argument in favor of planning.

ferent individuals cannot be foreseen, because these effects are spread far too widely and the rules themselves are intended to remain in force for a very long period, implies that in the formulation of such rules no deliberate choice between the relative need of different individuals or different groups need or can be made, and that the same set of rules is compatible with the most varied individual views about the relative importance of different things.

Now it must be admitted that this task of creating a rational framework of law has by no means been carried through consistently by the early liberals. After vindicating on utilitarian grounds the general principles of private property and freedom of contract, they have stopped short of applying the same criterion of social expediency to the specific historic forms of the law of property and of contract. Yet it should have been obvious that the question of the exact content and the specific limitations of property rights, and how and when the state will enforce the fulfilment of contracts, require as much consideration on utilitarian grounds as the general principle. Unfortunately, however, many of the nineteenth-century liberals, after they had satisfied themselves about the justification of the general principle which they had rightly refused to accept as a dictate of the law of nature, were on the whole content to accept the law in its existing formulation, as if this was the only conceivable and natural one. A certain dogmatism in this respect, which often had the appearance of an unwillingness to reason on these problems, brought the development of this kind of planning to an early standstill and has tended to throw the whole liberal doctrine into discredit.

"Planning" in the second, narrower sense, which is the only subject of discussion in our days, would be more accurately described, following the French term *économie dirigée*, as a system of "directed economy." Its essence is that the central authority undertakes to decide the concrete use of the available resources, that the views and the information of the central authority govern the selection of the needs that are to be satisfied and the methods of their satisfaction. Here planning is no longer confined to the creation of conditions which have their effect because they are known in advance and are taken into account in the decision of individuals. Regulations and orders are made with the intention of review, and change in connection with a change in circumstances, which, under the first type of planning, would simply have led to a changed response of the producers concerned. The foresight of the individuals is here no longer used to get every change in circumstances registered in the price structure as soon as anyone notices or expects such a change. The knowledge which guides production is no longer combined knowledge of the people who are in immediate charge of the various operations—it is the knowledge of the few directing minds which participate in the formulation and execution of a consciously thought-out plan. The only known mechanism by which the knowledge of all can be utilized, the price mechanism, is discarded in favor of a method by which the knowledge and the views of a few are consistently and exclusively utilized. It is planning in this sense which is today increasingly used when one industry is told not to exceed a certain limit of output or not to increase its equipment, when another is prevented from selling below (or above) a certain price, when the owner is forbidden to exploit a particular mine or to farm a specified acreage, when the number of shops in a particular branch is restricted or a producer is subsidized to produce in one place rather than in another, and in the infinite number of measures of a similar kind. And it is in particular planning in this sense which, as we shall see, every reorganization of society along socialist lines involves.

Now it is not intended to deny here that some amount of central planning of this kind will always be necessary. There are unquestionably fields, like the fight against contagious diseases, where the price mechanism is not applicable, either because some services cannot be priced, or because a clear object desired by an overwhelming majority can only be achieved if a small dissenting minority is coerced. The problem we are discussing is not, however, whether the price system must be supplemented, whether a substitute must be found where in the nature of the case it is inapplicable, but whether it ought to be supplanted where the conditions for its working exist or can be created. The question is whether we can do better than by the spontaneous collaboration secured by the market, and not whether needed services, which cannot be priced and therefore will not be obtainable on the market, have to be provided in some other way.

The belief that central planning in this sense is necessary to secure a more "rational" conduct of production in general—that is, to secure greater general productivity in some technical sense so that everybody would be better off—is, however, only one of the roots of the demand for such planning. It would be interesting, but it is not possible within the space available, to show how this belief is largely due to the intrusion into the discussion of social problems of the preconceptions of the pure scientist and the engineer, which have dominated the outlook of the educated man during the past hundred years. To a generation brought up in these views any suggestion that an order and purposeful reaction could exist which was not due to the conscious action of a directing mind was in itself "medieval rubbish," a piece of ridiculous theology which vitiated and discredited all conclusions based on such arguments. Yet it can be shown, in a manner which nobody who has understood the argument has ever contradicted, that the unconscious collaboration of individuals in the market leads to the solution of problems which, although no individual mind has even formulated these problems in a market economy, would have to be consciously solved on the same principle in a planned system.[10] Under the

[10] A beautiful specimen of this "scientific" prejudice occurs in the Foreword to *Planned Society* where Mr. Lewis Mumford speaks of the "sublime and now incredible theology: the conception that order is so far preordained in human affairs that a multitude of blind actions and reactions will bring it to pass." Yet while this is still the attitude of those brought up on popular science, it is essentially the more rigid "mechanist" view of the nineteenth century—there must be few eminent scientists now who are guilty of this dogmatism. At least in so far as biology and psychology are concerned even an outstanding "positivist" and eminent student of the methods of pure science like the late Professor Schlick recognizes a "general principle" that "frequently proves to be valid in psychology and biology; namely that the

price system the solution of these problems is impersonal and social in the strict sense of the term and we can only just indicate in passing the curious intellectual somersault by which so many thinkers, after extolling society as a whole as infinitely superior and insisting that it is in some sense more than a mere collection of individuals, all end up by demanding that it must not be left to be guided by its own impersonal social forces, but must be made subject to the control of a directing mind—that is, of course, in last analysis, the mind of an individual.

It is also not possible within the limits of this essay to show why this belief in the greater efficiency of a planned economy cannot any longer be defended on economic grounds. At any rate, recent discussion of these problems has at least thrown much doubt on this belief, and many advocates of planning are now content to hope that they will succeed in making such a planned system, in so far as formal rationality is concerned, come very near to the results of a competitive system. But it can be rightly said that this is not the decisive question. Many planners would be willing to put up with a considerable decrease of efficiency if at that price greater distributive justice could be achieved. And this, indeed, brings us to the crucial question. The ultimate

result of organic, unconscious or instinctive processes is frequently the same as what would have resulted from rational calculation" (*Fragen der Ethik* [1930], p. 72). Vilfredo Pareto, in an interesting and little noticed passage in his *Manuel d'économie politique*, p. 234, spoke of the equations which determine equilibrium in a market, and concluded that "if one really knew all these equations, the only means available to human powers to solve them would be to observe the solution given in practice by the market."

decision for and against socialism cannot rest on purely economic grounds, and cannot be based merely on the determination of whether a greater or smaller output of society is likely to be obtained under the alternative systems in question. The aims of socialism as well as the costs of its achievement are mainly in the moral sphere. The conflict is one of ideals other than merely material welfare, and the difficulty is that these conflicting ideals still live together in the breasts of most people without their being aware of the conflict. It is on considerations like those discussed here that we shall have to base our final choice.

It is undeniably true that planning in the specific sense, while it is not required to make production more rational in any formal sense, is required if the relative well-being of different people is to be made to conform to some preconceived order, and that a distribution of incomes which corresponds to some absolute conception of the merits of different people can only be achieved by planning In fact, it is only this argument of justice and not the argument of greater rationality which can be legitimately advanced in favor of planning. It is for this reason also that *all* forms of socialism involve planning in this specific sense. "Society" cannot take possession of all the material instruments of production without taking upon itself the decision of the purpose for which and the manner in which they are to be used. This is no less true under the systems of "socialist competition" which have been recently proposed as a solution of the difficulties of calculation under a more centralized system than under the older schemes of socialist planning.[11]

It must also be added here that planning of this kind, if it is to be done rationally and consistently, cannot long be confined to partial or local interference with the working of the price system. So long as state action is confined to supplement the operation of the price system by providing for certain collective wants, or by giving all the same security against violence or infectious diseases, this leaves the price system in its sphere intact. But once the state attempts to correct the results of the market and to control prices and quantities produced in order to benefit particular classes or groups, it will be difficult to stop halfway. It is not necessary to review the familiar economic arguments which show why mere "interventionism" is self-defeating and self-contradictory, and how, if the central purpose of intervention is to be achieved, intervention must expand

[11] I have no doubt that this statement will be violently contradicted, since many of my socialist friends believe, and have publicly asserted, that they have found a method by which collective ownership of the material resources and the impersonal direction of production can be combined. I have here neither space, nor is this the proper place, to explain in detail why I think that this belief is erroneous. It must suffice here to point out that even if the socialist managers of production were given the greatest amount of discretion compatible with the end that the income derived from the material resources should go to society, the decision as to the amount of equipment to be entrusted to a particular manager, as to the risks he should be allowed to take, and as to the directions in which he should be allowed to test the wishes of the consumers, must be reserved to the central authority. This means that the decision about the size and number of the separate enterprises, as well as the nature of the industries to be established and the goods to be produced, will be taken centrally. Even if in this decision the planning authority would attempt to follow only economic considerations, it will in last analysis be this authority which decides the nature and the quantity of the goods that are to be produced, and, therefor, the nature of the needs

[17]

until it becomes a comprehensive system of planning.[12] But it is relevant in this connection to underline certain sociological factors which operate in the same direction. Inequality is undoubtedly more readily born if it is due to accident, or at least to impersonal forces, than when it is due to design. People will submit to misfortune which may hit anyone, but not as easily to suffering which is the result of arbitrary decision of authority. Dissatisfaction with one's lot will inevitably grow with the consciousness that it is the result of human decision. Once government has embarked upon planning for justice's sake, it cannot refuse responsibility for anybody's fate. In particular it will not be able to refuse protection against the consequences of any change which are regarded as undeserved. But so long as there is any remainder of a free market every single change will always be to the detriment of some, although the result of progress will in the long run benefit all. There is, there-

that are to be satisfied. And, although I have carefully studied all the proposals for socialist systems which professedly avoid central direction, I have failed to find one where the ultimate decision about the use to be made of the available resources is not left to the essentially arbitrary decision of some central authority. The contrary impression derived from a cursory reading of these proposals is due to the fact that the crucial question of how it is decided what resources are to be given to an individual producer is usually left obscure or treated as if it were an insignificant administrative detail. Dr. O. Lange's recent study, *On the Economic Theory of Socialism* (Minneapolis, 1938), which has been acclaimed by some of the younger socialists as a real solution of the difficulty, amounts to nothing but an elaborate system of price-fixing in spite of an impressive scientific nomenclature. All the important questions remain unanswered (who is to do the price-fixing, at what intervals prices are to be fixed or revised, how the action of the managers is to be controled, etc.). A more detailed examination of such proposals must, however, be reserved for another occasion.

[12] Cf. L. V. Mises, *Kritik des Interventionismus* (Jena, 1929).

fore, no progress which somebody with an equity in the received ways of doing things would not have the interest to stop. The great advantage of the competitive system, however, lies exactly in the fact that it offers a premium on foresight and adaptability, and on the fact that one has to pay for it if one wishes to stay in an occupation which has become less needed. Any attempt to indemnify people against the consequences of changes which they have not foreseen makes the forces of the market inoperative and makes it necessary to put central direction in their place.

III

The wide popularity which the idea of central direction of all economic activity enjoys today is easily explained by the two facts that, on the one hand, people are promised by experts a greater amount of welfare if industry is "organized" along rational lines, and, on the other, that it is so obvious that those particular ends which each individual most desires can be achieved by planning. But if people agree about the desirability of planning in general, their agreements about the ends which planning is to serve will in the first instance necessarily be confined to some general formula like "social welfare," the "general interest," the "common good," greater equality or justice, etc. Agreement on such a general formula is, however, not sufficient to determine a concrete plan, even if we take all the technical means as given. The sad but undeniable fact is that all these formulas which are so freely used prove empty of content as soon as we attempt to use them as guides in any concrete decision as to economic planning. Economic planning always involves the sacrifice of some ends in favor of others, a balancing of costs and results, a choice between alternative possibilities; and the decision always presupposes that all the different ends are ranged in a definite order according to their importance, an order which assigns to each objective a quantitative importance which tells us at what sacrifices of other ends it is still worth pursuing and what price would be too high.

We only need to visualize for a moment the type of specific questions the planning authority will have to decide in order to see the ultimate issues involved. The planning authority would not only have to decide between, say, electric light for the farmer or bathrooms for the industrial worker in town, but it would also have to decide whether, if the installation of electric light in a hundred farms is regarded as more important than the provision of bathrooms for fifty working-class families, they ought still to give the preference to the claims of the farmers if instead they might have provided sixty working-class families with baths. The planner will not only have to know whether an additional doctor or an additional school teacher is more urgently needed, but he will have to know how to choose if, at the cost of training three doctors, he can train five teachers, and how if at the same cost he can train six teachers and so on. A decision whether a housing scheme in one town or another ought to be started first, or whether the greater costs of building in the one place are more than offset by the greater urgency of the needs there, a decision whether the cost of dispersing population to a certain extent is greater or smaller than the aesthetic and cultural advantages thereby obtained, can only be arbitrary—that is, there are within wide limits no grounds on which one person could convince another that the one decision is more reasonable than the other. Yet in making his decision the planner must give a preference, he must create distinctions of value or merit, and in a plan as a whole there is inevitably implied a whole scale of values. Agreement on a particular plan requires, therefore, much more than agreement on some general ethical rule; it requires much more than adherence to any of the ethical codes which have ever existed; it requires for society as a whole the same kind of complete quantitative scale of values as that which manifests itself in the decision of every individual, but on which, in an individualist society, agreement between the individuals is neither necessary nor present.

The idea that a completely planned or directed economic system could and would be used to bring about distributive justice presupposes, in fact, the existence of something which does not exist and has never existed: a complete moral code in which the relative values of all human ends, the relative importance of all the needs of all the different people, are assigned a definite place and a definite quantitative significance.[13] If such a complete

[13] To this statement only egalitarianism, in its strictest and most mechanical interpretation, constitutes an exception. If we could agree that all persons, old or young, healthy or sick, men or women, industrious or idle, were to be given the same money income to be spent as they please—it would probably have to be the same income in terms of commodities—we would have a definite rule to guide us. But the mere wish to approach greater

code, which it is difficult even to conceive, were in existence, then planning would indeed raise few political difficulties. But no single mind is comprehensive enough to form even an individual conception of such a comprehensive scale of human aims and desires. And still less has there ever been or can there ever be agreement on such a code between a number of individuals, not to speak of agreement between a majority of all. But only to the extent that such agreement exists can we speak of the existence of such ethical code. Such a complete code as would be required in a completely directed economy would in effect have to decide for every human action how it was to be taken. No known religious or moral code—at least among civilized people with a high degree of differentiation between individuals—has even to any limited extent approached such a system.

This idea of a complete ethical code—indeed, the idea of any differences in comprehensiveness of different moral codes—is somewhat unfamiliar.[14] That there are

---

equality provides no serviceable guide. Even if we agree that everything which we take from the rich to give to the poor means a social gain, we have not yet decided to whom the spoils are to go. The formula of the approach to equality is as empty as that of the "common welfare," the "social good," etc.

[14] The ideal of a complete moral code which comprehends all the needs of all people and gives them their definite value helps, incidentally, to clear up an old confusion about the meaning of "self-interest" and "egotism" in economic analysis. All that is presupposed in the "individualist" approach is that in the scale of values only a limited number of objectives and only some needs of some other people will and can have a definite place, and that a comprehensive scale does nowhere exist. It makes no difference for analytical purposes whether in the scale of values of an individual only his own physical needs or also those of a number of other people have a definite place. It may also be pointed out that what is commonly called "egotism"

questions which when they are raised are "moral" questions, but to which "morality" has no answer, where there are no given values on the basis of which to decide, and where such values would therefore have to be deliberately created if the question were to be answered, is an idea to which we have yet to accustom ourselves. Yet it is the problem which is inevitably raised by the suggestion that unified direction of individual activity should be used in the service of social justice, and we must beware of minimizing a difficulty because it is of a character with which we are not familiar. The fact is that on questions of this sort, because they have so far not constituted a problem for anyone, there has been no occasion to seek an answer, and still less has there been occasion for a common opinion to arise concerning them. Only when we try to make explicit in deliberate discussion and decision that which formerly was decided by chance, or at least by impersonal market forces, can these questions be rationally answered, and all the actions of the members of the planned society will have to be guided by the answer.

Before leaving this subject it should at least be indicated that the development of human civilization in the

----

and "altruism" does by no means correspond with the narrowness or comprehensiveness of the individual scales of values. The "altruist" is very frequently the person who feels the distress which he sees so much more than that of which he only knows intellectually that he is very willing to sacrifice those of whose needs he only knows by hearsay to those whose suffering he has under his eyes. *Ce qu'on voit et ce qu'on ne voit pas* has its moral side, and those whose vivid sensation of the suffering they see makes them impatient to relieve it by any means may often be much more egotistic (in the sense of narrowness of their scale of values) than the cool reasoner who takes the indirect effects of a particular measure into account.

past has been accompanied by a movement from (in this sense) more to less comprehensive moral systems. From the member of the primitive tribe, whose daily life is a succession of acts regulated by a firmly established ritual, to the individual in the feudal society, whose fixed status determines the claims on life to which he is entitled, down to our own times development has been toward a life in which a constantly widening area was governed by individual taste and preference. The change made necessary by central planning would require a complete reversal of this tendency by which moral—and legal—rules have for centuries tended to become more formal and general, and less specific.[15]

But our question here is not whether we ought or ought not to have such a complete and comprehensive moral code which would provide a generally acceptable basis of planning for social justice. The question is whether anything approaching such a complete code exists—that is, whether most people, or even only those who are regarded as the best and wisest by the others, agree at least on the major problems of value which an attempt to plan would raise. And there can be no doubt that the answer to this is negative, that where such moral rules will be needed they cannot be found but will have to be created.

[15] This is not to say that a somewhat too rapid emancipation from traditional moral and religious belief may not be partly responsible for the mental instability of our generation. There can be little doubt that the existence of firm tradition has materially helped to preserve free institutions in the Western world, just as its absence has contributed to their downfall in Central Europe. But the essential point here is probably that the coercive apparatus of law should cover a narrower field than the rules of morals and tradition, and that great caution should be exercised in going beyond it.

IV

These excursions in what may seem remote specula-
tions on questions of moral philosophy are not without
relevance to our concrete problem. We can now return
to the question of what happens when a democracy be-
gins to plan, and shall find that these general considerations find an immediate application here. The fact that
a measure of agreement, which does not exist in a free
society, is required in order to translate the apparent
agreement on the desirability of planning into concrete
action has two important consequences. In the first
instance, it is responsible for the conspicuous inability
of democratic assemblies to carry out what is appar-
ently the expressed will of the people, because it is only
when the vague instructions have to be translated into
specific action that the lack of real agreement manifests
itself. The second effect of the same cause, which ap-
pears wherever a democracy attempts to plan, is the
recognition that if efficient planning is to be done in a
particular field the direction of affairs must be "taken
out of politics" and placed in the hands of permanent
officials or independent autonomous bodies. This is usually justified by the "technical" character of the decision to be made, for which the members of a democratic
assembly are not qualified. But this excuse does not go
to the root of the matter. Alterations in the structure
of civil law are no less technical and no more difficult to
appreciate in all their implications; yet nobody has as
yet seriously suggested that legislation should here be
delegated to a body of experts. The fact is that in these

fields legislation will be carried no farther than the general rules on which true majority agreement can be achieved. But in the direction of economic activity—say of transport, or of industrial planning—the interests to be reconciled are so divergent that no true agreement on a single plan can be reached in a democratic assembly. Any decision here involves the direct and conscious choice between the satisfaction of particular needs of one group of people and that of another. There will often be a great many slightly affected in one way, and a few affected in another. If action were dependent on the agreement of a numerical majority, no action could be taken. But, in order to be able to extend action beyond the questions on which true agreement exists, the decisions are reserved to a few representatives of the most powerful "interests."

But this expedient of "delegation" is not effective enough to placate the dissatisfaction which the impotence of the democracy must create among all friends of extensive planning. The delegation of special decisions to numerous separate organizations presents in itself a new obstacle to proper co-ordination of the plans in different fields. Even if, by this expedient, democracy succeeded in planning every sector of economic life separately, it would still remain impotent with regard to the larger task of a comprehensive plan for all the sectors taken together. Many special plans do not yet make a planned whole; in fact, as the planners ought to be the first to admit, they may be worse than no plan. But the legislature will be naturally reluctant to delegate decisions on really vital issues. In the end agreement that planning is necessary, together with the inability of the democratic assembly to agree on a particular plan, must strengthen the demand that the government, or some single individual, should be given powers to act on their own responsibility. It becomes more and more the accepted belief that, if one wants to get things done, the responsible director of affairs must be freed from the fetters of democratic procedure.

That the increasing discredit into which democratic government has fallen is due to democracy having been burdened with tasks for which it is not suited is a fact of the greatest importance. It has not yet received adequate recognition. Government by agreement is possible only if government action is confined to subjects on which people have common views. If we decide first that it must act on a certain question and inquire only afterward whether agreement exists on how it should act, we may find that we shall either have to coerce people to agree, or to abandon government by agreement, or both. And the farther the scope of government action extends, the greater the likelihood that this situation will arise. The fundamental position is simply that the probability of agreement of a substantial portion of the population upon a particular course of action decreases as the scope of state activity expands. There are certain functions of the state on the exercise of which there will be practical unanimity; there will be others on which there will be agreement of a substantial majority—and so on until we come to fields where, although every individual might wish the state to intervene in some direction, there will be almost as many views about how the government should act as there are different persons.

Democratic government worked successfully as long as, by a widely accepted creed, the functions of the state were limited to fields where real agreement among a majority could be achieved. The price we have to pay for a democratic system is the restriction of state action to those fields where agreement can be obtained; and it is the great merit of the liberal creed that it reduces the necessity of agreement to a minimum compatible with the diversity of individual opinions which will exist in a free society. It is often said that democracy will not tolerate capitalism. If "capitalism" here means a competitive society based on free disposal over private property, it is far more important to observe that only capitalism makes democracy possible. And if a democratic people comes under the sway of an anti-capitalistic creed, this means that democracy will inevitably destroy itself.

If democracy had to abdicate its control over economic life, this might still be regarded as a minor evil compared with the advantages expected from planning. Indeed, many of the advocates of planning fully realize —and have resigned themselves to the fact—that if planning is to be effective democracy, in so far as economic legislation is concerned, has to go by the board. Mr. Stuart Chase believes that he can reassure us that "political democracy can remain if it confines itself to all but economic matters."[16] It is, however, a fatal delusion to believe that authoritarian government can be

[16] Quoted by Walter Lippmann, *Atlantic Monthly*, December, 1936, p. 729.

confined to economic matters. The tragic fact is that authoritarian direction cannot be restricted to economic life, but is bound to expand and to become "totalitarian" in the strictest sense of the word. The economic dictator will soon find himself forced, even against his wishes, to assume dictatorship over the whole of the political and cultural life of the people. We have already seen that the planner must not only translate the vague and general "ends" that command popular approval into a concrete and detailed scale of values, but he must also, if he wants to act at all, make the people believe that the particular detailed code of value which he imposes is the right one. He is forced to create that singleness of purpose which—apart from national crises like war—is absent in a free society. Even more, if he is to be allowed to carry out the plan which he thinks the right one, he must retain the popular support—that is, he must at all costs appear successful.

It is in vain to blame the dictator who has been carried into power by the universal wish for consistent and energetic use of the powers of the state if he uses this power to make the people's wishes and ambitions fit into his plans. "Rational" action is only possible in the service of a given system of ends, and if society as a whole is to act rationally it must be given such a common scale of values. The dictator will find at a very early stage that if he wants to carry out the will of the people he will have to tell them what to want. We need not go to authoritarian countries to find instances of this tendency. Not very long ago Mr. Henry A. Wallace found it necessary to warn the American people "that a steadfast national allegiance to any fixed course, international or intermediate, also requires a certain degree of regimented opinion."[17] What can we expect from a man who has to organize a nation for the execution of one gigantic plan if this is the lesson which a responsible statesman draws from the comparatively moderate experiments in planning made by the United States? If there is no activity and no human relation which is not regulated by the state, how can opinion about these things be left free?

The decision of the planner about the relative importance of conflicting aims is necessarily a decision about the relative merits of different groups and individuals. Planning necessarily becomes planning in favor of some and against others. This is in effect admitted by all the authoritarian governments when they insist upon the predominance of politics over economics; and it has been explicitly stated by one of the leading sociologists of present-day Germany. He writes:

Planning means the highest degree of taking sides for and against the various forces and interests, a long-run commitment in favor of one side or the other. . . . . The fact that planning means taking sides in the struggle of interests is only obscured by representing particular individual interests as the interest of the whole. . . . .[18]

The problem here, of course, is not that the different people concerned have not the most decided opinions about the relative merits of their respective wishes; it

[17] *America Must Choose*, "World Affairs Pamphlet" (New York: Foreign Policy Association, 1934), quoted by Lawrence Sullivan, "Government by Mimeograph," *Atlantic Monthly*, March, 1938, pp. 306–7.

[18] Hans Freyer, *Herrschaft und Planung* (Hamburg, 1933), p. 19.

is rather that these opinions are irreconcilable. But the ground on which the more or less arbitrary decision of the authority rests must seem to be just, it must appear to be based on some ultimate ideal in which everybody is supposed to believe.[19] The inevitable distinction between persons must be made a distinction of rank, most conveniently and naturally based on the degree to which people share and loyally support the creed of the ruler. And it further clarifies the position if to the aristocracy of creed on the one end of the scale there corresponds a class of outcasts on the other, whose interests can in all cases be sacrificed to those of the privileged classes.[20]

Conformity to the guiding ideas cannot, however, be regarded as a special merit—although those who excel by their devotion to the creed will be rewarded. It must be exacted from everybody. Every doubt cast upon the rightness of the ends sought or the means chosen is apt to diminish loyalty and enthusiasm, and must therefore be treated as sabotage. The creation and enforcement of the common creed and of the belief in the supreme wisdom of the ruler becomes an indis-

[19] This is the real function of the "political myths" which the unwitting pupils of Sorel are so fertile in inventing. The myth of *"Blut und Boden"* is the basis of a whole system of agricultural policy and the myth of the "corporative state" a most convenient cloak to impose a new hierarchical order upon society.

[20] The suffering of the racial or national minorities does not begin with the totalitarian regimes. How completely in the modern interventionist state the idea of equality before the law has lost its meaning could be easily shown by a discussion of the treatment of minorities in various democratic European states since the war. It has been amply demonstrated that it is possible to wage incessant economic warfare against a particular group and completely to destroy the basis of its economic life without in the least infringing the letter of the laws or treaties guaranteeing the rights of minorities.

pensable instrument for the success of the planned system. The ruthless use of all possible instruments of propaganda, and the suppression of every expression of dissent, are not accidental accompaniments of a centrally directed system—they are essential parts of it. Nor can moral coercion be confined to the acceptance of the ethical code underlying the whole plan. It is in the nature of things that many parts of this code, many parts of the scale of values underlying the plan, can never be explicitly stated. They exist only implicitly in the plan. But this means that every part of the plan, in fact every action of the government or its agencies, must become sacrosanct and exempt from criticism.

It is, however, only the public expression of criticism that can be forcibly suppressed. But doubts that are never uttered and hesitation that is never voiced have equally insidious effects if they dwell only in the minds of the people. Everything which might induce discontent must therefore be kept from them.[21] The basis for comparisons with conditions elsewhere, the knowledge of possible alternatives to the course taken, information which might suggest failure on the part of the government to live up to its promises or to take advantage of opportunities to improve the lot of the people, all these must be suppressed. There is consequently no field where the systematic control of information will not be practiced. That the government which claims to plan economic life soon asserts its totalitarian character is

[21] "Whilst the work is in progress, any public expression of doubt, or even of fear, that the plan will not be successful, is an act of disloyalty, and even of treachery, because of its possible effect on the wills and on the efforts of the rest of the staff" (Sidney and Beatrice Webb, *Soviet Communism*, p. 1038).

[32]

no accident—it can do nothing less if it wants to remain true to the intention of planning. Economic activity is not a sector of human life which can be separated from the rest; it is the administration of the means with which we seek to accomplish all our different ends. Whoever takes charge of these means must determine which ends shall be served, which values are to be rated higher and which lower—in short, what men should believe and strive for. And man himself becomes little more than a means for the realization of the ideas which may guide the dictator.

Perhaps it is not unnecessary to add here that this suppression of individual freedom is not so much the result of the transition from democracy to dictatorship as both are the result of the enormous expansion of the scope of government. While undoubtedly democracy is to some extent a safeguard of personal freedom, and while its decline is due to the very fact that it makes the suppression of freedom more difficult, our problem is not mainly one of constitutional change in the strictly political sense. There can be no doubt that in history there has often been much more cultural and political freedom under an autocratic rule than under some democracies—and it is at least conceivable that under the government of a very homogeneous and doctrinaire majority democratic government might be as oppressive as the worst dictatorship. The point is not that any dictatorship must inevitably eradicate freedom, but that planning leads to dictatorship because dictatorship is the most effective instrument of coercion and enforcement of ideals, and as such is essential to make central planning on a large scale possible. A true "dictatorship of the proletariat," even if democratic in form, if it undertook to direct economic activity would probably destroy the last vestiges of personal freedom as completely as any autocracy.

VI

It is to be feared that to a great many of our contemporaries this picture, even if it should be recognized as true, has lost most of the terror which it would have inspired in our fathers. There have always been many, of course, to whom intellectual coercion was only objectionable if it was exercised by others, and who regarded it as beneficial if it was exercised for ends of which they approved. How many of the exiled intellectuals from the authoritarian countries would be only too ready to apply the intellectual coercion which they condemn in their opponents in order to make people believe in their own ideals—incidentally furnishing another illustration for the close kinship of the fundamental principles of fascism and communism? But, although the liberal age was probably freer from intellectual coercion than any other age, the desire to force upon people a creed which is regarded as salutary for them is certainly not a phenomenon that is new or peculiar to our time. What is new is the attempt on the part of our socialist intellectuals to justify it. There is no real freedom of thought, so it is said, because the opinions and the tastes of the masses are inevitably shaped by propaganda, by advertising, by the example of the upper classes, and by other environmental factors which relentlessly force the thinking of the people into well-worn grooves. But if, the argument proceeds, the ideals and tastes of the great majority are determined by factors which are under human control, we might as well use this power to turn their thoughts into what we think a desirable direction. That is, from the fact that the great majority have not learned to think independently but accept ideas which they find ready-made, the conclusion is drawn that a particular group of people—of course those who advocate this—are justified in assuming for themselves the exclusive power to determine what people should believe.

It is not my intention to deny that for the great majority the existence or nonexistence of intellectual freedom makes little difference to their personal happiness; nor to deny that they will be equally happy if born or coaxed into one set of beliefs rather than another, and whether they have grown accustomed to one kind of amusement or another. It is probably only too true that in any society freedom of thought will be of direct significance or will exist in any real sense for only a small minority. But to deprecate the value of intellectual freedom because it will never give everybody the same opportunity of independent thought is completely to miss the reasons which give intellectual freedom its value. What is essential to make it serve its function as the prime mover of intellectual progress is not that everybody may think or write anything, but that any cause or any idea may be argued by somebody. So long as dissent is not actually suppressed, there will always be some who will query the ideas ruling their contemporaries and put new ideas to the test of argument and propaganda. The social process which we call human reason and which consists of the interaction of individuals, possessing different information and different views, sometimes consistent and sometimes conflicting, goes on. Once given the possibility of dissent, there will be dissenters, however small the proportion of people who are capable of independent thought. Only the imposition of an official doctrine which must be accepted and which nobody dares to question can stop intellectual progress.

Perhaps it must actually be seen and appreciated in one of the totalitarian countries to fathom how completely the imposition of a comprehensive authoritarian creed stifles all spirit of independent inquiry, how it destroys the sense for any meaning of truth other than that of conformity with the official doctrine, and how differences of opinion in every branch of knowledge become political issues to be decided by the intervention of authority. Experience indicates, however, that there are still many who are ready to sacrifice intellectual freedom because it does not mean the same opportunity for all. Surely they do not realize what is at stake. Indeed, the great danger comes from the fact that we take the inheritance of the liberal age for granted, and have come to regard it so confidently as the inalienable property of our civilization that we cannot fully conceive what it would mean if we lost it. Yet freedom and democracy are not free gifts which will remain with us if only we wish it. The time seems to have come when it is once again necessary to become fully conscious of the conditions which make them possible, and to defend these conditions—even if they should block the path to the achievement of competing ideals.

The danger which our generation faces is not merely that the process of experimentation—to which we owe all progress in the social sphere as elsewhere—should lead us into error. The danger is rather that by error we may bring the process of experimentation itself to an end. If the experiment of planning leads to the disappearance of free institutions, there will be no opportunity for the correction of that mistake. Once the only method of peaceful change yet invented, democracy (that admirable convention of "counting heads in order to save the trouble of breaking them"), has gone, the way for a peaceful correction of an error once committed is blocked. Those in power, who owe not only their position but also—and more significantly—the opportunity to realize their ideals to this error, will not recognize it as such and will therefore not correct it; and nobody else will have a chance. With an altogether unwarranted optimism a recent writer predicted that, within a generation, the "planners" and all their works will be swept away by a violent revulsion of feeling if the material stability they promise has to be bought at the price of intellectual and spiritual oppression.[22] It must appear highly doubtful, in view of the unprecedented power over the minds of the people which the modern techniques of propaganda give to the state, whether a reversal of intellectual tendencies through forces from inside the organized group will still be possible once the

 D. Mitrany, in *Planned Society*, p. 662.

machinery for control has been firmly established. It is more likely that the struggle for the survival of ideas will then take the form of a war of ideologies between nations, which, even if it should lead to the survival of the most efficiently organized group, may well mean the destruction of everything which to us represents the greatness of humanity.